Dudley`s Castle

Written by
David R. York

Illustrated by
Moran Reudor

Copyright © 2024 David R. York
www.corenology.com

All rights reserved. No part of this publication may be reproduced, distributed, or transmitted in any form or by any means, including photocopying, recording, or other electronic or mechanical methods, without the prior written permission of the publisher, except as permitted by U.S. copyright law. For permission requests, contact the author at david@corenology.com.

Published by Redwood Publishing, LLC
www.redwooddigitalpublishing.com
Orange County, California

ISBN: 979-8-9906149-2-5 (hardcover)
ISBN: 979-8-9906149-4-9 (paperback)
Library of Congress Control Number: XXX

Illustrations (cover and interior): Moran Reudor
Layout: Creative Publishihing Book Design

To speak with the author directly about bulk purchases or author talks, please contact him at david@corenology.com.

Not every gift can be given,
nor can every treasure be stolen.

Steward (noun):

A person who puts hard work and effort into something bigger than just themselves.

NOT long ago, in a land not far away, stood a mighty gray castle perched atop a lush green hill. The castle was surrounded by a busy, vibrant village that hummed with the sounds of banging hammers, clanging pots, and busy people. The colorful village, in turn, was ringed by a thick rock wall, which brought comfort to those within, and gave pause to those without. The land outside the walls flourished with a variety of neatly planted crops, orchards heavy with fruit, and livestock lazily grazing in their pastures.

INSIDE the great castle there lived a spirited young boy named Dudley. Dudley's days were filled with adventures befitting a child and his friends. There was no pretend enemy of the village that they could not defeat before the sun came to rest each day. While the foes may have been imagined, the battles were real and the victories sweet. Dudley lived in the castle with his father, who Dudley saw as the king of the village, not to mention the wealthiest man in all the land. This brought Dudley no small measure of pride.

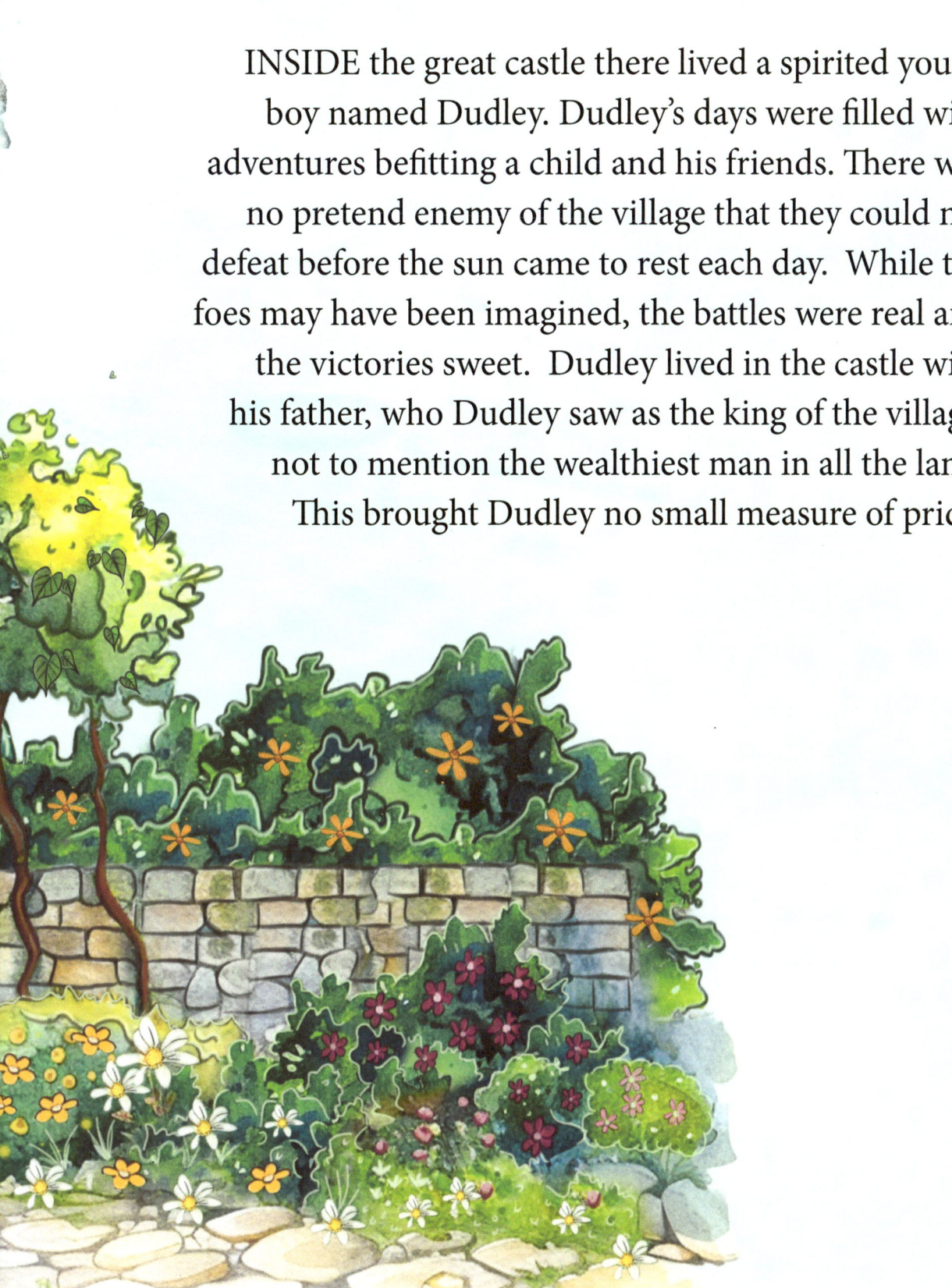

THE CASTLE was not without its mysteries. Legend told tales of vast riches held deep within a hidden vault. Dudley and his friends spent countless hours reading about grand adventures and in turn dreaming of all that the treasure could buy for them if they could find it. Large sailing ships. A stable of swift horses. Supplies and resources for grand adventures far and wide. Despite diligent searches by Dudley and his friends for the entrance to this secret vault, or even a clue to its whereabouts, the treasure remained undiscovered and undisturbed.

WHEN not vanquishing foes or searching for treasure, Dudley spent his time walking the village and grounds with his father. Dudley's father knew the weight of each rock, the length of each timber, and the stitch of each tapestry. He patiently shared every detail of the castle, as well as the village and its walls, while Dudley impatiently listened. They talked with the merchants of the marketplace, built what seemed like miles of livestock fencing, and studied agriculture and crops. Dudley felt that all these lessons were somewhat beneath a boy who would one day become king. Nevertheless, Dudley considered himself to be the wealthiest lad in the most enchanted place.

ON DUDLEY'S eighteenth birthday, his father sat him down to share the truth. Leaning back in his leather-bound chair, Dudley's father explained: "My son, contrary to what you might think, I am not the king of this castle. Rather, I serve as its steward. As such, I am responsible for the castle and all its resources, but I am not its owner. This means that as much as I may want to, I cannot leave to you the riches it contains. Doing so would make me a thief. If you wish to obtain the wealth these walls protect, you must first build your own castle, one that is worthy of holding the treasures of this place. Then you may return here, and I will give you the riches hidden within."

DUDLEY, determined more than ever to acquire wealth for himself, ventured out to build a castle of his own. The journey was fraught with trials. He climbed mountains that scraped the sky, cut through dense forests that tested his will, and crossed wide, dangerous rivers. The days were hot and long, and the nights were cold and longer. Hunger and thirst became his only traveling companions. The comfort of the castle seemed like a distant dream as Dudley trudged through an untamed, unkind world.

AFTER MONTHS of difficult travel, Dudley came upon a peaceful hillside. Standing by a creek at the base of this hill, he finally saw a place that he could call his own. But dreams are one thing and reality quite another. Along his journey, he had learned some difficult lessons about the vital necessity of shelter, fire, water, and food. Throughout the work of each day, he would think about the long walks he'd taken with his father and the lessons his father had tried to teach. Now, as fantasy faded and reality set in, his father's words about crops and seasons, tools and materials, and the nature of … well … nature, were slowly beginning to make sense.

DUDLEY started humbly: a small creaky cottage with a leaky roof, a muddy well, and a garden that did not produce much food. But over time, his efforts began to transform the land. Dudley expanded the cottage and made the gardens bloom. He visited neighboring towns, where he traded his increasing crops for much-needed materials and know-how. He met carpenters who taught him the song of the chisel, stonemasons who showed him the art of sculpting rock, and blacksmiths who spoke to him through forged iron.

DUDLEY'S years of tireless effort finally resulted in the completion of a new castle and village worthy of his father's wealth. Dudley looked upon his creation with pride. But amid the splendor, a loneliness clung to the ornate rooms and vast courtyards. He'd realized his vision, but his heart was still empty. The castle was rich in stature yet poor in wealth. At least for now.

DETERMINED to at last claim the treasure he had longed to possess, Dudley returned to his childhood home. Reuniting with his joy filled father, Dudley recounted all that had happened. Dudley spoke of the hardships he had endured, the skills mastered, and the magnificent new castle. He shared how the beauty of what he'd dreamed of had made him work all the harder, and that hard work, in return, had brought beauty to life. He then spoke of the void that persisted: the emptiness of that castle, which still needed to be filled with treasures.

HIS FATHER then took Dudley to the castle's highest spire and looked down at the bustling village. His father closed his eyes and reveled in the sounds below. "I told you long ago that I was not the king of this castle, but rather its steward," his father explained. "In truth, as its steward, I am something more. You see, if you are not very careful, *everything you think you own will actually own you in return*. Possessions can possess us, and blessings can become a curse. The purpose and the people are the treasure of this place."

AFTER PAUSING for a moment, his father continued, "I also told you I would not be a thief. What you did not know was that it was you whom I thought of robbing. You see, we can sometimes steal from people when we give them things but keep the cost for ourselves. I did not want to rob you of the trials of your journey, as they would give your castle its worth. I did not want to steal from you the tools and wisdom you would gain from building your castle, as they would teach you how to care for it and make it flourish. Most of all, I did not want to take from you the purpose for your work or the treasures you choose to fill it with."

AS DUDLEY leaned forward on the spire's open window, his father continued sharing. "I was once you. Long ago, I stood on a lonely hill and sought to build my name and wealth. Fortunately, along the way, I learned that true riches are gained from the lives we touch and the love we share. The best treasures any castle can ever hope to contain are those that are hidden in plain sight, where they can be seen, enjoyed, and experienced each day."

FINALLY understanding all that his father had sought to teach, Dudley returned to his castle and threw open its gates, inviting artisans, farmers, scholars, and families from near and far. He shared with them the fruits of his land and the beauty of his efforts. The castle, once a symbol of his personal triumph, transformed into a cradle of people and purpose. Standing in an archway and soaking in all the hustle and bustle of life, Dudley closed his eyes and listened to its myriad sounds. From that moment on, he no longer owned the castle, for he had become its steward.

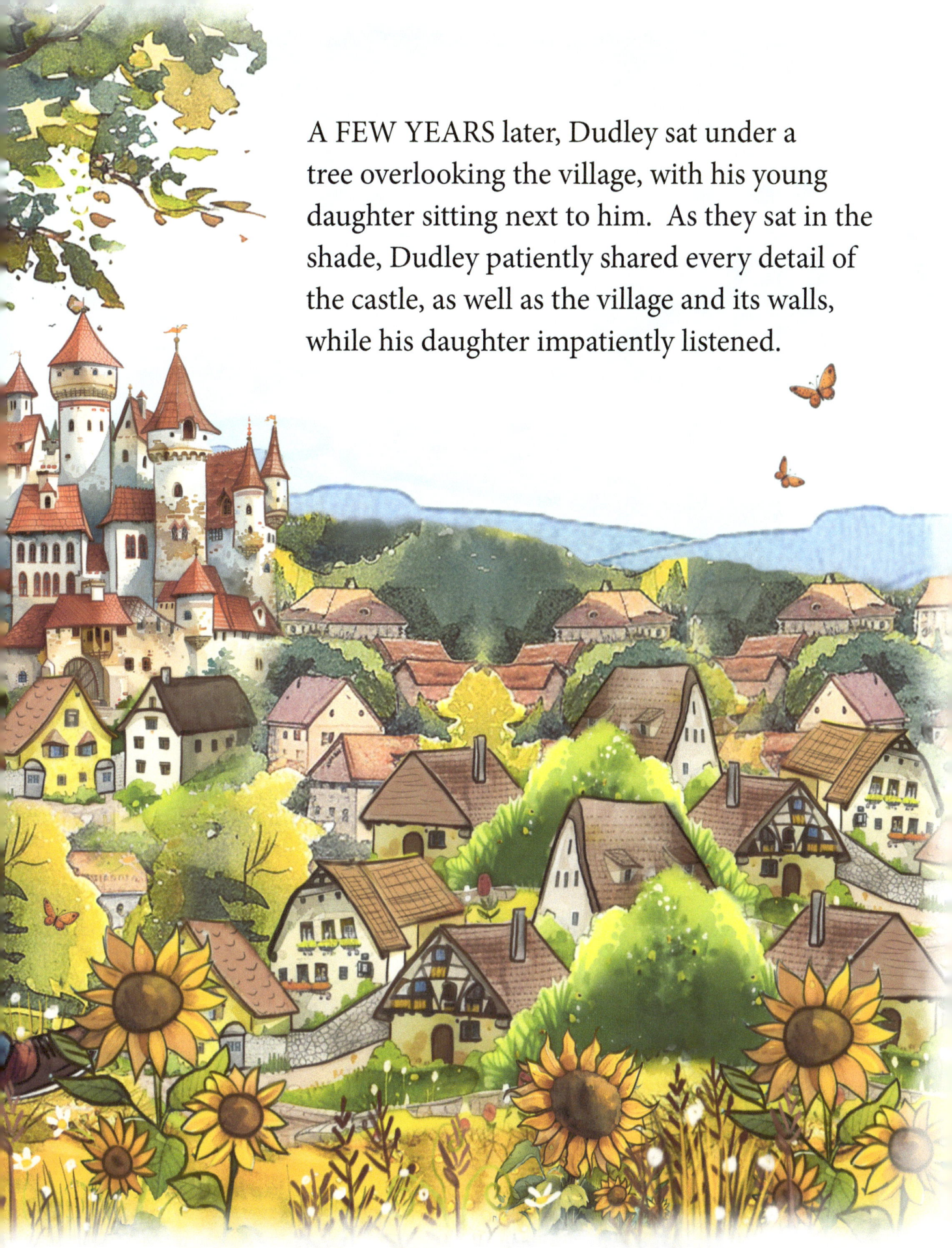

A FEW YEARS later, Dudley sat under a tree overlooking the village, with his young daughter sitting next to him. As they sat in the shade, Dudley patiently shared every detail of the castle, as well as the village and its walls, while his daughter impatiently listened.

Questions to Consider

1. What does it mean to be a steward? How does Dudley learn to become a steward throughout the story?

2. How does Dudley's character change from the beginning of the story to the end? What important lessons does he learn along the way?

3. Why does Dudley's father make him build his own castle before giving him the key to the treasure? What does Dudley learn from this experience?

4. What does Dudley's father mean when he says, "True wealth is not measured in gold or stone, but in lives changed and love shared"? How does this idea change Dudley's view of wealth?

5. What challenges does Dudley face on his journey to build his own castle? How do these challenges help him grow?

6. How does opening his castle to artisans, farmers, scholars, and families change Dudley's life and his castle? Why is community important in the story?

7. At the end of the story, Dudley begins to teach his daughter the lessons he learned. Why is it important for Dudley to pass on these lessons? How might his daughter benefit from them?

8. Can you think of a time when you had to work hard for something important? How did that experience help you grow, and what did you learn from it?

9. What are the treasures in your life?

10. Think about something you can do right now that could impact you and those around you for the better. How can you put it into action?